I0494189

How to SELL a Home That Didn't Sell the First Time

Dana C. Trumann

This book is dedicated to:

JOC Alex P. Haley, USCG, Ret.

*CDR Joseph P. Dunn, USN. MIA South China Sea,
February 14th, 1968*

Contents

Acknowledgments

The following people have been instrumental in helping me develop as a real estate agent in my first ten years of the business, and will no doubt influence me in the next ten:

From the Craig Proctor organization in Toronto, Canada: Craig Proctor, Willie Miranda & Tammi Johnson. Not that I think you guys really deserved a gold medal in Olympic Hockey for men & women for a third straight Winter Olympics, but I'll get over it. Your record is almost as impressive as the US winning the gold in hockey against the Soviet Union in Lake Placid, NY, 1980!

Dan Kennedy, Robert Kiyosaki.

Arthur Gary of the Arthur Gary School of Real Estate.

I'm lucky to have been influenced by you all.

Thanks to Spike for editing this book. Without you, it would still be a stack of papers.

Foreword

It is my hope that if you are a home seller, this quick read will help you avoid having a home "expire" on the market, and that if you are an agent you will become more successful in your career of helping people sell homes. We as real estate agents are the cornerstone of the American Dream (with a nod to Canadian Agents) and few people know how hard we work to serve our clients. I am honored to be one of YOU.

1
FIFTY PERCENT FAILURE!

A few years ago when Donald Trump's show "The Apprentice" was relatively new, and network TV wasn't competing with Netflix and YouTube, I was fortunate to attend a real estate agent seminar co-sponsored by Donald Trump and Wells Fargo. "The Donald" had recently released a book about the best real estate advice he had received, and one of the contributing writers, a man named Rich Casto, was the guest speaker that day. The point Rich made that stood out to me the most was that, typically, half of the homes that get put on the market fail to sell. This conference was pre-real estate crash of 2008, and my first real estate sale was an "expired" that I got an offer on in one day, so the concept struck a chord with me, and is the focus of this book. If you are a home seller and want to be on the winning side of the fifty percent, this book is for you and will help you choose the right agent. If you are an agent and want to increase your effectiveness and efficiency when it comes to helping people sell their homes, then keep on reading because you are benefiting from more than ten years of intense real estate coaching and training from the best real estate trainers and coaches in North America!

2
PICTURES

Here is a twist on the old adage, "A picture is worth a thousand words." When we apply that to real estate, "A picture is worth thousands of DOLLARS," and pictures can be what keep your house from selling if they are of poor quality. With the majority of home buyers in the US and Canada starting the home-buying search online, it is becoming more important to show a house in the best possible way, using good photography as well as PLENTY of photos to tell the story of the home. Many homes that expire on the market never had a chance because the agent didn't get good quality photos, nor placed the maximum number allowed on their respective Multiple Listing Service Sites (MLS). Since more and more MLSs syndicate (send and share) property information and photos with consumer-focused websites – for example, Realtor.com, or company based sites such as Remax.com, ExitRealty.com, ColdwellBanker.com, etc. – consumers are quite often narrowing the choices of properties they want to see prior to speaking to an agent about seeing properties, meaning they have already disqualified a bunch of the homes based on the photos. No longer is using a low-grade digital "instamatic" camera suitable to represent a seller's home. Even our fine iPhones (I've been using one since '07) that take good pictures aren't up to the task when there are thousands of dollars at stake. If you want to play at this level of the game, your two choices are either: shell out the cash to buy a pro-quality 35mm digital camera (I use a Nikon) with a wide angle/zoom lens if you only want to buy one lens – the lenses alone cost more than the typical "one shot" digital camera... or pay to have a professional photographer come out and take pictures of the home with their PROFESSIONAL camera (which is probably a Nikon or Canon...).

With good QUALITY photos, don't forget good QUANTITY – if the local MLS will support 35 pictures, put 35 pictures on, not 34, not 30, not 10. I am constantly amazed by how many homes (and I don't mean the truly ugly/tear down/put your McMansion on this lot) even as I write this are expiring on the market and don't have the maximum number of photos allowed on the site. And remember the part about syndicating to other sites? Realtor.com, Remax.com, ExitRealty.com, etc., won't be showing the maximum number either because they get the information directly in most cases from the MLS, not the agent. Lose. Lose.

3
VIDEOS

Here is another tool that most homes' sellers don't have working for them, not due to outrageous cost anymore, but rather just lack of know-how or execution on the part of the agent.

A few years ago I was one of the "cool kids" in my market to pay a photographer to take pictures of properties I was selling and also create "virtual tours," which were a moving slide show connected to cheesy music that gave a perspective buyer a reason to spend more time looking at a house online. It wasn't an inexpensive thing to do. It did help my clients' properties attract more attention, which equaled more showings, more offers, and a quicker sale than if I didn't, so it helped grow my referrals from satisfied sellers. In 2009 I upgraded to a much better (more expensive…) website that had a do-it-yourself Virtual Tour feature, so now I didn't have to pay a photographer to make them with cheesy music, I had my own cheese music built into my website.

Meanwhile, as the Virtual Tour offer as a menu choice for potential sellers helped our business, YouTube had been expanding beyond surf & skate videos (that I and fellow surfers/skaters watched and shared with each other) and all kinds of other entertaining or goofy videos that folks shared, mainly due to the fact that Google had purchased them back in 2006. As I saw YouTube transition from a fun/entertaining site to one rich in educational content with lots of "how-to" videos, from learning how to play Don Gibsons' "Sea of Heartbreak" to changing the oil in my 2000 Harley Davidson FXDX, I transitioned our property videos to YouTube as well. Utilizing YouTube has helped push our property listings higher up the Google food chain as far as being able to find properties we are selling, which has in turn helped get the properties sold. Some agents use a very elaborate process to create and process the videos, some (like me) just get out to the property and give you a walk around view to get a sense of the home beyond the still photos we also supply. No comment on my lack of Movie Star looks or my odd speaking cadence and syntax – at least I was one of the early adopters in my market!

Another plus is that you can watch YouTube videos on your TV through that Wii system you got for Christmas a few years ago for the exercise programs…

4
AGENT WEBSITES

I remember from early in my career how easy it was to blow thousands of dollars getting an agent website up and running, and, you know, you needed a website because real estate was moving online! It was easy to spend a lot of money promoting the website too, and it seemed like there were and still are people ready to sell an agent a quick fix to solve their online puzzle. Good luck with that!

The problem with most of the websites then and now is they are typically online business cards that don't really provide much value to the consumer, but at least they have dropped in costs, and some companies do provide "free" ones to their agents.

So where does the agent website fit in regard to helping SELL a clients house?

a) The site should provide relevant real estate buying and selling content that is useful for the consumer.

b) Putting your client's home on this site with useful information increases the likelihood of the home being seen by a potential buyer – remember, the home will be on the MLS in addition to the consumer-accessible sites, but since we are looking for ONE buyer for the house, more sites mean more chances of the home being seen.

c) If you are updating a blog on your site that discusses relevant real estate or neighborhood info for the area that the property is in, it can increase property views – the site will rank higher in Google searches if the blog content is congruent with the neighborhood. The trick here is to be consistent with blog updates, posting a minimum of once a week, which most agents don't get to. Subcontracting the blogging task is done by some agents to keep pushing new content on the site, but the challenge is whether or not it is neighborhood/town specific – remember, we are trying to show this home to people who are interested in homes in the town.

d) If the agent is utilizing a pay-per-click advertising campaign on Google, offering homes to buyers in the town the house for sale is in, there will be more folks seeing the house.

e) Mobile website access allows consumers that see a sign rider on the "for sale" sign on the property to utilize their smartphone to get information on the home for sale – the key is to have a mobile site in addition to your standard site, so that the consumer can see the relevant information of the home on their mobile device, instead of a scrunched-up version. We pay extra for our website to have this feature, but it is a cost we are willing to cover in order to increase the likelihood of selling the home.

5
SIGNS

Property signs let people walking or driving by a home know that it is for sale. The signs work 24 hours, don't call in sick, aren't late, and don't require a staff of technicians to operate, although in some areas they may need someone to shovel the snow away so they can be seen.

A post sign system costs more, as opposed to a smaller metal frame 'stick in the ground' with a smaller sign panel, but the additional height usually improves visibility, and requires fewer snow removal sessions.

With the shift away from the "normal" 9-5 business world, how do you solve the problem of a consumer standing in front of the house you are selling and calling the number on the sign looking for property info? If the real estate office provides a live receptionist, what happens when a call comes in at 5:01PM? The consumer might leave a message, but more likely will just get annoyed and hang up and forget about that house. Did not sell!

One solution would be to pay for a 24-hour answering service, which I have done, but when testing it at 2 a.m. I found myself on hold for more than 5 minutes… not good.

In the previous chapter where we discussed websites, we mentioned "sign riders" that would provide steps for a consumer to get instant information about the house from their smartphone, and also be able to get the information without having to talk to someone with horns coming out of their head if they just wanted to get some info. You see, most consumers don't want to talk to a real estate agent in the initial stages of house hunting – they want to go at their own pace, and when they are ready then they will ask for an agent's help. Since most agents don't sell many homes, they tend to be in a hurry and want to rush the consumer through the process, as opposed to giving them time to go through it on their own. I have heard that when a person does not have to contact an agent to get property information, sign inquiries increase by 200 to 400 percent. When someone inquires about one of our properties for sale with their smartphone through our text sign riders, they get the information sent to them via our mobile site, and we get notified about their inquiry. We tactfully follow up with the inquiry on the property to make sure the person got the information they were looking for, rather than try to SELL the home to them. If they are interested in seeing the home at the time of the call, then great, we have another chance at selling the home. If not, we follow up after a time to see if they may be interested in seeing the home, which gives us another opportunity to sell the home.

6
Brochure boxes

Okay, now we get to the teamwork part of this book!

While smartphones are becoming more prevalent, not everyone carries one. The lack of a cellphone does not necessarily indicate a lack of affluence.

A brochure box can replace some of the attributes of a text or call sign rider by at least giving the consumer information about the home for sale. Property specifics, photos, and agent contact information can be placed on these brochures, giving the consumer an easy way to get more information.

A couple of downsides to the brochures:

a) It can be embarrassing for a potential buyer to pull alongside a house in a neighborhood, park, get out, walk (with ALL the neighbors starring – you know they are!) over to the brochure box, and then find it empty. When they slink back into their car, you can bet they will not have had much of a positive experience to associate with the property. If the agent can provide plenty of brochures for the seller to have as back stock, and the seller maintains an adequate supply in the brochure box, then a brochure box may be a good marketing touch for the house. KEEP THE BOX FULL!

b) Since most brochure boxes aren't waterproof, rain does damage the brochures, and if you don't replace them, the consumer gets an ugly pamphlet of your house. Maybe okay, but most likely not how we want to do things. Once again, if the seller is okay with replenishing after the rain has passed and things have dried out, this may be a good piece of marketing to add to the mix.

If the house is vacant or if you as a seller don't want to bother with replenishing the stock of brochures, then you run the risk of both A and B above, because your agent may be justifiably too busy to visit your home several times a week to monitor this system. An empty or messy brochure box is worse than no brochures at all. If the seller and agent can take a team approach to maintaining this marketing piece, then add it to your mix!

7
CLEANING THE HOUSE

My house is not ready for people to come in to see if they want to buy it. Between kids, rescue dogs, rescue cats, and my wife and me working, it is a struggle some days to find my reading glasses if I put them down in one of the stacks of papers throughout the house my wife calls "Dana piles." And so what if I smoke my pipe while my wife is away for a few days and the aroma lingers? That is ok, my house isn't for sale – this book is about you and yours!

If your house is marketed effectively and you are priced accordingly, you will have people coming to check it out. Once they are there, if there are foul smells from animals (remember the part about me having critters?), people smoking (but pipes smell good, I keep saying....), etc., you will have a harder time getting your price, or maybe the person won't even bother writing an offer because they are to annoyed by the smell. I remember when a buyer barfed in the basement of a home we were showing because a dog decided use to use that basement as a bathroom rather than go outside right before we got to the house. That person did not write an offer.

Please remember I'm just trying to be helpful with these tips. I am not throwing stones from my Old New England (not glass) Farm House, aka Dana's Perpetual Fixer-Upper!

We have a saying in the real estate business: "Kitchens and bathrooms sell houses." I'm not going to argue.

Here are some additional tips:

a) Make the house look good from the outside – we want an inviting approach. Cut the grass, sweep the sidewalk and driveway, pull weeds, water the grass, trim the bushes, clean the gutters, make sure the flowers look good – or if you are dealing with winter weather, try to have the walkways to the house clear, snow shovels stowed neatly, de-icing pellets/salt on steps, etc.

b) Get rid of clutter in the house: have a yard sale, donate things to Goodwill or other charities, give stuff to friends that aren't selling their homes anytime soon. If you don't really use it, do you want to bring to your next home? If you do want to keep your "stuff," then putting things in storage while the home is on the market is another option.

c) Replace or repair leaky faucets. Just do it.

d) Replace the shower curtain.

e) Make sure all lights are working – stove, basement, attic, garage – not just the obvious areas.

f) Don't have pets or any pet related items visible or on site during a showing, if at all possible. Some folks have no sense of humor when it comes to critters. We have a standing rule that we won't work with people that don't like animals. Really. But you need a buyer for your house.

g) Paint walls that need it. Be safe and go with egg shell white as a rule of thumb.

h) De-personalize the home. Family photos can interfere with a potential buyer seeing themselves in the home. Put them in a box, because you are moving soon, okay?

If your home has more of an elaborate layout with lots of fancy furniture, art, or other unique features, you may want to consult with a staging professional – think of them as an interior decorator focusing on increasing the desirability of your home in the eyes of a potential buyer. The investment in professional staging is of more strategic importance the higher up the affluence ladder the home is segmented in.

8
PRE-INSPECTIONS

This is the key to making your home sale boring. When you are in the middle of a real estate transaction, boring is good. The four key areas of real estate that can cause a sale to not happen are:

a) During the initial offer, can the two parties decide on a price?
b) If there are material defects of the property discovered during the inspection phase, can the parties agree on pricing or repair concessions?
c) Can the buyer's financing hold together until the sale is final?
d) Will the property appraise at the agreed-upon sales price?

A pre-inspection minimizes the effect of item B that a buyer's inspection during the due diligence phase can have. Having to re-negotiate the purchase and sale agreement because the inspection unveiled issues with the plumbing, heating, structural integrity, roofing, etc., is avoidable. If a seller has the home pre-inspected prior to bringing the house to market, issues can be dealt with in advance, repairs can be made, or the issues can be made known and be part of the transaction, basically saying "here is the house, and this is the price, warts and all." Avoid a surprise that will cost the seller in dollars and stress during the transaction. Boring is good.

9
NEWSPAPERS

"Why advertise in the newspaper when everyone starts their home search online?"

"Newspaper advertising is dead."

Okay, so I know advertising in the newspaper can be expensive. I stumbled into being a "listing agent" in the early stages of my business with a expired listing, got it under contract in one day, and haven't looked back, BUT it can be expensive representing sellers versus buyers. If you work with buyers, you need two things: a cell phone and a car. If you want to work with sellers you need a bunch more tools, more than I am going to address in this edition of the book.

WHO reads newspapers is a good question. As far as demographics go, Baby Boomers, Leading Edge Boomers and Seniors are the groups most likely to buy and read newspapers.

Another interesting fact about these groups is they tend to skew higher on the income and asset side of things versus younger age groups. Hmmmm.

We are looking for the ONE buyer for this home, so it might make sense to look for that buyer among a group of people that spend money to get their news and information on a consistent basis.

When it comes to newspaper advertising, I am more in favor of advertising in a paper that costs the reader money as opposed to the free weekly ones, but being in both increases the chance of selling the home, which is what this book is about.

Avoid falling under the spell of the internet being the only media needed for selling houses: it is just one piece of the puzzle.

10
AGENT LICENSE LEVELS

I have been known to quote the statement, "for $300 you can ruin someone's financial life," meaning that the process of getting an entry-level real estate license isn't very challenging compared to other fields that don't have the same income potential.

When it comes to selling your home you may want to stack the odds in your favor and get the highest level licensed agent you can. I'm licensed in Maine, and we have 3 levels: Sales Agent, Associate Broker, and Broker. After taking a 55-hour course and completing a couple of other steps, you can be licensed as a Sales Agent. One long work week with overtime gets you the keys to the kingdom! What this means is the person fresh out of class could be the one trying to sell your home. To be fair, the agent is supposed to be supervised while conducting real estate activities. Typically that is done by the "Designated Broker" who is the Licensee all the other agents in the office answer to, but sometimes that person might be busy working on their own deals, and just might miss one teeny weeny aspect of the deal the new agent is working on (selling your house?), which could cause a crisis in your life.

Here is what happened to me as a new agent:

I got a referral from a person whose house had expired on the market, and while it was on the market and empty, the agent hadn't checked on the home after a big rain storm. Yup, the power had gone out, the sump pump stopped working, and the basement (full finished – nice floors, walls, etc.) flooded. Anyway, the seller came back to the state and cleaned out the basement, but was running out of money and needed to sell the house fast because they had already been transferred to a different state and needed to get rid of the house before the bank foreclosed. I put it on the market and got it under contract the first day, and things looked good – I was a Hero, The Man and all that. Of course the offer was reviewed by another agent since I was new and didn't really have any idea of what I was doing now that I was in the real world of real estate. The other really neat thing about this deal was that my client told me he wasn't going to have to pay the real estate commission – his company would, due to the job transfer, which was good because at this point he just had enough money to get back to his new place and was basically broke. I'm looking really good now. Nod your head in agreement.

And then my world went sideways.

Here is what went wrong for me as a new agent with required supervision: We accepted an offer that was contingent upon financing, not cash, and the day they would be able to actually purchase the home was after the foreclosure date. We weren't getting calls from other buyers so we really had to work with these buyers, the finance company, etc. to get there financing pushed up to close before the clock ran out. It looks easy as I type this, but in reality it was a struggle.

The other exciting piece that I didn't need was when my client's employer (a Maine-based company, established in 1884, with a global maritime reach) was notified of the deal we were trying to do to avoid foreclosure. They told us that the client had been mistaken: the company didn't pay commissions up front (a few thousand dollars that my client did not have), but rather would reimburse the seller after closing. Me on the phone to the company: "Would you be willing to make an exception this one time?" Them: "No, it is against company policy." So here I was as a new agent trying to fix both of these issues, and the management of the company I was at didn't quite know how to fix them, but somehow I as a rookie agent did manage to hold everything together with the financing people, as well as get the client's company to make an exception regarding their handling of commission payments with regards to real estate transactions. These two mistakes now seem silly compared to the bigger challenges I have had to face in later years of being a real estate Broker & Team Leader, but as a new agent I hadn't developed the skills to prevent or sense these kinds of problems. Regardless of whatever a state's requirements are for newly licensed real estate agents, you have to ask yourself if you really are prepared to place what could be your most valuable asset in the hands of an inexperienced person.

The mid-level license here is Associate Broker, which you are forced to upgrade to after 2 years as a Sales Agent or 3 years with a waiver. When I took it we had to take 2 separate courses, pass them, and then take a state exam. This license level is the one most active/career focused agents have. The requirements to maintain the license are for agents to take a defined number of continuing educational credits on an ongoing basis.

The top license is Broker. There is no requirement to advance to this level, so since there is a time, effort, and money expenditure to get this extra "stripe", most people don't bother.

This is the license that is held by the agent that answers to the state when it comes to following real estate commission guidelines.

When you need a lifesaving operation do you want the doctor right out of school cutting you open, even though they will be supervised during the operation?

If you are facing a legal calamity, do you want the attorney just out of law school handling your case, even though they will be supervised by a senior attorney?

When it comes to selling your most valuable asset, why wouldn't you want the highest-level licensed person representing you?

11
COLLEGE

A college degree is not required for one to become a real estate agent.

In the book "The Millionaire Mind," written by Thomas Stanley, there is a segment that covers higher education – seems like most American millionaires did attend college (90 percent) and receive a Bachelor's degree with an average 2.92 GPA. A theory that I came across a few years ago was that when a person went on to even higher levels of college education, Master's degrees, PHDs, they were less likely to become wealthy. They surmised that when a person received a graduate or higher level degree, they were less likely to do less stimulating (meaning grunt work) within a business to build it up. Hmmmm. Something for me to jibe my attorney buddies about.

There are many successful real estate agents that have not bothered to go to college, and I have personally paid money to be coached by some of them.

After I spent 8 years in active duty in the US Coast Guard

(directly from high school to boot camp), I was motivated to learn. I enrolled full-time at a community college and was able to compress my schedule in order to complete a two-year degree (Associate's) and obtain a year-long certification in outdoor education within two years.

As time went on, more business opportunities presented themselves, and in some situations I felt "under-gunned," so I decided to get my Bachelor's degree in night school. This was a very un-fun period of life since I also had 3 kids in school, a full-time job, owned a full-time business and was still in the Coast Guard Reserve. It was a two-year program that took people with the equivalent of an Associate's Degree, and two years later you would have your Bachelor's. Most people would go to school full-time to get this, so since it was part-time you can probably imagine the heavy amount of studying involved. We had a bunch of people drop out of the program.

In spite of the "hassle" I and many other people experience when attending higher education once we have hit adulthood, the end result is that I am a better businessman because of it, and believe that other people that have gone down this path would agree they are better business people because of the experience.

As in the preceding chapter, you may feel that a higher level of education is important when it comes to selling what could be your most valuable asset. In my experience you don't pay a higher fee to an agent because they have a degree.

12
PEOPLE IN UNIFORM

You may have bought this book because your home didn't sell, and now you really want to get it sold.

A real estate transaction is one of the most stressful situations that a person can be involved with, close to a few other stressful life experiences: Birth, Death, Marriage, Divorce.

When you are in the process of selling your home, your agent needs to be comfortable telling you the truth even if it makes you angry. Working with sellers seems to invite more opportunity for disillusionment (maybe not lavishing praise on you as their agent during the process) as opposed to working with buyers, for many factors.

a) Sellers tend to see their homes as being more valuable than the buyer, so getting the price they hoped for may not be in line with the market.

b) Many sellers are selling a house in order to buy another home simultaneously.

c) There can be many psychological anchors to the home that trigger emotional responses during a negotiation – maybe a buyer comments on being annoyed that they have to paint over the growth lines you marked in a door jamb to show how fast your kid was growing, maybe they comment dismissively on the choice of wallpaper you and your significant other spent four weekends together putting up.

d) "This home was good enough for me to raise my family in, who does this idiot think he is complaining about X?"

You want your agent to be able to help you through these potentially trying periods and not get upset with you because you may not be "at your best" while dealing with the emotions that can show up during a transaction. You want an agent with "thick skin" who is mission-focused, that knows within a few days after the sale you will be back to your normal nice self!

Folks with a background in high stress jobs can provide the additional fortitude you want during your home selling process: police, fire, medical, or military, to name a few.

13
MARKET DATA

Most agents are trained in and utilize a Comparative Market Analysis (CMA) to determine the price to put a home at on the market. However, since real estate markets are rarely balanced, and are usually shifting toward a buyers' market or sellers' market, we may have a situation arise where the value we have come up with doesn't mesh with what an appraiser comes up with.

An appraiser is a professional whose sole purpose is to determine the value of a piece of real estate, so that they can advise a bank how much money they should put at risk when providing a loan to a buyer. We as agents wear many hats when serving a real estate client, and may not be in tune with values as much as an appraiser is – or even if we are more knowledgeable about the value of a particular piece of property, it can be challenging to "win" when going up against one if there is a dispute over value. The bank is usually the client of the appraiser.

A buyer and seller can come to an agreement on price and terms and condition of the property (two of the four areas where deals are made or killed, you may recall), but if the appraiser feels the property is worth less than the agreed upon purchase price, and the buyer can't or won't make up the difference, then the only option may be for the seller to reduce the asking price to fit within the loan terms the buyer is able to perform in.

There are times when it is worth spending the money on an appraisal to come up with a market price, rather than relying on a CMA exclusively.

A feature we have added to the services we provide sellers is an in-depth weekly market activity report for the town we work in, which keeps our clients in touch with market movement, inventory levels, and so on. The data is compiled by a third party and is not influenced by us in any way, which gives our clients a desirable unfair advantage when it comes to knowing what the market is really doing.

14
Solo Agent vs. Teams

There are several real estate agent models and teams available for the consumer to choose from. When an agent advertises that they have sold 200-plus homes in a previous year, or that they have sold four times the number of houses that an "average" agent sells, does that mean that they will do a better job of selling your house than another agent? Not necessarily.

Here are a few points to consider when choosing an agent to sell your house.

a) Do they specialize in your neighborhood? If you take a quick scan of most agents' websites, they will tell you that they specialize in this town, and another, and another, and on and on. REALLY? How can you specialize in a bunch of towns? How can you be the EXPERT? Do you want heart surgery performed by a heart surgeon that is also a brain surgeon that is also a bariatric surgeon that is also a colon & rectal surgeon…? You get the point. NO. If you want to sell your house, make sure the person really specializes in your town. It's okay if you want to experiment and go against my advice, but when your home doesn't sell, then how about trying my way?

b) Are they primarily a buyer agent or a seller agent? Earlier in the book I mentioned the tools a buyer agent needs. A phone, and a car. This is typically where new agents begin their real estate careers. The tool kit for sellers encompasses many more piece$$$. You remember the thing about weekly statistical updates, call capture/SMS sign riders, town-specific websites with Google pay-per-click campaigns pushing your home in front of buyers, manually putting town-specific info into their blog, newspaper ads of your home, postcards sent to local home owners (oops, next chapter for the postcards), and so on? Make sure the agent specializes in working with home sellers.

c) Has the agent's business matured to the point where they are more particular about who they will work with? Maybe they have reached a point where they have a balanced life and aren't concerned with sales awards and will refer most potential buyers and sellers to other agents? They may be the be the best agent to get the job done.

When it comes down to it, I think that what is important is that the agent working for you has great systems in place to sell your home, AND a full time administrative person that works hand in hand with them. If an agent has a buyer agent or many buyer agents on the team, I think the direct benefit to you as a consumer is negligible. If you price and market a property properly, it is difficult to keep the home a secret, so all the other buyer agents in the market place will be glad to bring their buyers to the house, meaning they can all be working to get the job done.

15
TELLING THE NEIGHBORS

Since there is a good chance that one of your neighbors would love it if one of their friends were able to move into the neighborhood, the chance of your home selling increases if the agent sends out "Just Listed" postcards to the neighborhood.

Your home will most likely be put on the MLS when you list it with an agent, and even though it will syndicate with consumer websites, it doesn't mean the neighbor we are looking to help us sell the home will see it online. If you are selling a condo there may be rules against using a real estate For Sale sign, so the next best thing is making sure postcards get mailed to the neighborhood.

If your agent invests in an information hotline, the card could have that number with a specific extension on it, giving a caller access to automatic information about the home beyond what you could fit on the postcard.

16
"That's what I'm paying you for!"

Silly me! I remember learning a little marketing piece at a real estate training event in Orlando one January, which I implemented as soon as I got back to Maine – you get a business card made up with the photo of the house for sale on one side, and the other side gives pricing and contact information. You give a stack of these to your client, and anytime they are out and about and maybe start talking to someone about having their house for sale, they give out one of their cards and ask the friend to give it to another person if they aren't interested in it.

Well, one of the clients we made these for was angry that we expected him to have anything to do with selling his house, since he was paying us. Okay, no problem. I paid for the cards, and besides the stack we were going to give him we had already dropped some off at area businesses – gas stations, coffee shops, the post office – all within his town.

This type of person is not a good candidate for filling their brochure box either....

17
CONCLUSION

I hope you have found this book valuable and informative. Get out there and sell your house! This book is a living document and will be updated. Check out www.DanaTrumann.com to stay up to date on the most powerful techniques you can use to sell your house, even if it didn't sell the first time.

Thank you for reading!

www.ingramcontent.com/pod-product-compliance
Lightning Source LLC
Chambersburg PA
CBHW070723180526
45167CB00004B/1594